THE ART OF MOTHER- HOOD

KAREN STUBBS

Requests for information should be addressed to:
iDisciple, 13560 Morris rd, suite 1140, Alpharetta, Georgia 30004.

ISBN 978-0-9992813-3-8

CONTENTS

I dedicate this book to my children,
Kelsey, Emily, Taylor, and Abby.

I love looking at each of you and seeing the masterpiece that God is creating. I am humbled to have played a part in your story. Thank you for forgiving me when I messed up as a mom, for loving me always, and for each being so special to me in your own way. I love you.

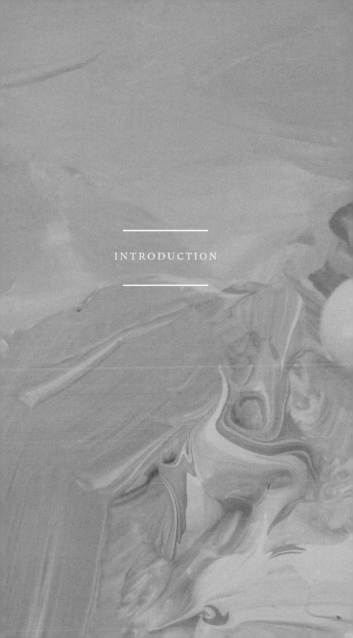

INTRODUCTION

And we know that in all things God works
for the good of those who love him, who have
been called according to his purpose.

ROMANS 8:28

———

Good morning! I say good morning because it is morning as I write here in Georgia, and I just poured a cup of coffee and sat down to begin a conversation with you. I would love to sit at your local coffee shop with you, dear mom, and hopefully put your mind at ease about being a mom. When the going gets rough, we moms often say to ourselves, "I'm a bad mom." When we tell ourselves that—and I say "we" because I have been guilty of it too, more times than I can count—it does something to us. So as a veteran mom of 28 years, I would love to buy you a cup of coffee, look into your beautiful face, and say,

"You are <u>NOT</u> a bad mom! *You are a great mom, a mom who is doing an incredible job of raising your children!"*

I would love to give you a big hug and tell you that you just need to relax a little bit.

Why would my "words" of encouragement even matter? Well, because like I said, I am a veteran mom of 28 years, which means I'm old and with age you gain wisdom. If you are like me, I like talking to older people about raising children, because they understand, they "get it" and have "been there." Trust me, I've been there! I have four grown children, Kelsey, Emily, Taylor and Abby. I am now a grandmother. So I know about motherhood. I married my husband Greg right after I graduated from college (Auburn University in case you were wondering), and after four years of marriage we started our family with the birth of Kelsey. I was probably a lot like you in those early years. I wanted to be a great mom, the best mom, but I didn't have a clue as to what I was doing. A lot of days, not every day, but a lot of days I felt like I was missing the mark in motherhood. I wasn't sure what the "mark" was, but my children didn't always obey, I tended to lose my cool and not be patient all the time, and my house wasn't a picture of perfection. Sound familiar? But, when my children went to play at other people's homes, the moms would tell me they behaved and had good manners, so that was positive and at times I would see a glimpse of behaviors changing and my children would make the right decision.

"AND WE KNOW THAT IN ALL THINGS GOD WORKS FOR THE GOOD OF THOSE WHO LOVE HIM, WHO HAVE BEEN CALLED ACCORDING TO HIS PURPOSE."

ROMANS 8:28

Through all those years of raising children, my husband traveled, and most weeks, months, years, I did the parenting thing by myself. Greg would call in and see how things were going, he was interested in and cared deeply about the family, but he is a pilot, and pilots travel. That left me in the trenches by myself. At first, I was frustrated by having to do it alone, and gave into the idea that it wasn't fair; but then, I realized that attitude and mindset wasn't getting me anywhere except for being angry and in a bad mood all the time. I eventually matured and realized that whether it was fair or not, it was my life. I married a pilot and that is the way it is. I decided to "suck it up buttercup," and get to parenting. Even in those days of having a better attitude, I still went to bed some nights thinking I didn't do a great job in the mommy department that day.

Now my children are grown, and I'm here to tell you that even though I did mess up a lot of days, there was always love in our home. Even though their dad traveled all the time and missed key events some years like holidays, birthdays or special programs, my children still love and adore their father. I guess I can honestly say that God ended up making it all for the good, just like He promises us in His word (Romans 8:28). That is why I wanted to write this book. That is why I would reach across the table from you if we were having coffee and say, "Sweet mom, breathe! You are doing a great job and your efforts are not in vain. Hang in there, keep doing what you are doing and don't give up!"

Obviously, the whole coffee shop scenario won't work. And as you read this book, imagine that we are having a conversation. I'm not going to pretend like I know everything about being a mom, because I don't. I'm not going to write out several chapters on the "how to" of motherhood. Instead, I'm just going to have a conversation with a few friends, sharing what I have learned over the years, throw in some encouragement, and hopefully point you to Someone who does have all the answers, who is an expert and has been my mainstay in this journey of motherhood. I bet you know who I'm talking about—our heavenly Father and His Son, Jesus.

Before we talk about motherhood, I want to share with you a realization that I had last May on a mission trip. God met me one morning in Costa Rica. It wasn't while I was having my quiet time, or while I was loving on the Costa Rican children. It wasn't anything that profound. Rather, God met me in a hallway while I was painting a mural. It was a quiet meeting. His voice was very soft, and I almost missed it, but I'm glad I didn't, because this realization was powerful. Isn't that the way God is a lot of the time? He meets us in the morning while we are nursing our baby, or gives us discernment when disciplining our child, or shows us what grace looks like when we are parenting our teens and they don't deserve our grace. That is what makes God so amazing, so loving and long suffering. I used to wonder, what does "long suffering" mean? Then I became a mom, and realized that motherhood is the epitome of long suffering.

The definition of <u>long suffering</u> is *having or showing patience in spite of troubles, especially those caused by other people.*

Whew! Can I get an amen up in here! Amen, to experiencing troubles caused by other people! Our children cause us lots of troubles. Trouble when they break our favorite coffee mug by running in the house when they are not supposed to. Trouble by lying to their teacher and embarrassing us as a mom, trouble when they wreck the family car. I could go on and on, but I won't because I know you understand exactly what I'm saying. In a mom's world, we practice long suffering every day, but so does our heavenly Father with us. How many times has God given me grace when I didn't deserve it? How many times has He been gentle with me, patient with me, meeting me where I am in motherhood? Too many to count.

Before I share with you my realization, let me share with you a story that will give you the background. I know, you want to hear the punch line, but the punch lines are always better after you hear the story. Plus, if we were really having coffee, I would for sure share my story with you, because I'm a storyteller. My story begins on a kindergarten field trip.

Art is not my "thing".

Growing up in Atlanta, I went to a small Christian school. On Valentine's Day, my kindergarten class took a field trip to Lenox Square. This field trip was different than most field trips, because it was an art competition. My class was told we would be participating in a Valentine Drawing Contest with other schools in the Atlanta area. I had been practicing with my mom at home, learning how to draw a heart. I was having a hard time drawing a heart. I could get one side, but the second curve of the heart was difficult for me to draw for some reason. As much as mom and I practiced, I could not "get" it. Therefore, if I'm honest, it made me anxious just to think about it.

Our class walked into the big plaza at Lenox Square, and there were easels with large poster boards set up throughout the open air plaza. To me, as a kindergartner, it looked like thousands of easels. As each of us found the easel we wanted and prepared to start drawing, I could feel my anxiety rising. The reality of the situation was, there was no way out, I had to try and draw a heart and I knew I couldn't do it, and even at five years old, I felt very inadequate and anxious.

The buzzer rang and everyone started drawing. As I looked around, it looked like everyone else's picture was coming together, but mine wasn't. Tears flooded my eyes. Suddenly, out of the corner of my eye, I saw my best friend, LeGay Coleman, running across the plaza to see what I had drawn. On my easel were a few attempts at half of a heart. LeGay, in her bold way, asked, "what's wrong?" I started crying and said, "I can't do it! I can't draw a heart." She said, "Sure you can!" Then she grabbed my crayon and drew a big heart, then turned it into a heart house with heart windows and a heart door. She told me to fill it in with grass and flowers, and promised that it would look great. Then she ran off as fast as she had come. I didn't win, but LeGay saved the day!

Fast forward to fifth grade, at a different private Christian school. The father of one of the students in my class was an illustrator for the Atlanta Journal-Constitution, and he worked a deal with the school to give free art classes to the fifth grade every Friday. We were all so excited, and each of us got our own sketch pad with pencils. The first day of lessons, he told our class that everyone can draw. Some may be better than others, he said, but everyone can draw. He would assess where each of us was and go at our speed.

I took art lessons my entire fifth grade year, and I tried. I REALLY tried. Every week I had great reports from my teacher on my performance as a fifth grader, except that I talked too much and I had a bad attitude concerning art. My teacher even sat me down and told me I was not trying hard enough. She was sure that if I tried harder, I would be a good artist. Once again, I cried. I told her I really was trying. At the end of the year, we took a field trip to a water wheel. Our end-of-the-year project was to sketch the water wheel. I was halfway through mine when the AJC artist walked behind me, bent down, and said to me, "Karen, I do not think you are a good artist. I know you are trying, I can see it, but this is not your thing, sweetie. It's okay, I know you will be good at other things in life." Once again, a few tears.

Fast forward a bit more, and now I am a mother. My

children over the years would ask me to draw a picture for them: "Mom, can you draw a dog?" And I would do my best, and then they would reply, "what is that, mom?" I would reply, "It's a dog, like you asked." They would reply, "No, it's not. I'll get dad to help me." No tears. I had developed thick skin by this age.

I am now an adult and know and realize that we can't all be good at art, and I'm okay with that truth. I am good at other things in life. Usually, art never comes up in my day-to-day world, and if it does, I can easily avoid it. There was a time, however, when I was on a mission trip with my family, when I could not avoid art, and that is where my story begins.

Mission Trip Group

COSTA RICA

CHAPTER ONE

The Master Painter

*For I know the plans I have for you,"
declares the Lord, "plans to prosper you
and not to harm you, plans to give you hope
and a future.*

JEREMIAH 29:11

May of 2017, I went on a mission trip with 32 college students to Costa Rica to minister to children who are living in poverty. We worked in the schools and undertook several beautification projects to make the facility more inviting. Since I was a leader, I knew the students wanted to be with the children, so I volunteered to be on the painting team. (I assumed we were just painting walls a solid color, which I can do!) On our first day I was introduced to Alfredo who was the man in charge of the art project, and he reminded me of Maui from the movie Moana. At first, I thought he was just a painter, you know the kind of painter that paints your house. But, as we got started, I realized Alfredo was not just a painter, he was in fact an artist.

Before we started the project I walked over to Al-fredo and asked him what was the plan of what we were doing. His reply was strange to me, he didn't tell me exactly what we were going to paint, he just said, "I have the plan in my head." I thought, *okay, cool, but why won't he tell me what the plan is.* Then he took our team of five to a long wall inside the school building, located on a ramp going to the second floor, and he said, "this is where we are going to paint." That's when I started to get a little nervous. I looked around to see who was on my team. My husband, Greg—I knew he could draw pretty well because when we were on a mission trip in Uganda he drew pictures on the walls of another school. In addition, we had a girl who was studying art at the University of South Carolina, the leader of our trip (Lee), and two college girls. I instantly convinced myself they were all amazing artists and began to feel inferior. I realized that we would not be rolling a wall changing the paint color, but we were doing a lot more than that. We were going to paint a mural, a very large mural, one that the children would look at everyday as they walked down the hall. I began to feel that I was on the wrong team. I am NOT an artist and should be in the classroom watching the little children. I felt insecure in my artistic ability and instantly felt like I was the weakest link. But, I couldn't change teams, I was on the painting the mural team, and Alfredo began. Alfredo took a red

Alfredo and Me

COSTA RICA

pencil and drew three lines on the massive wall from one side to the other. He instructed Greg and Lee to paint the top blue, and he told me to paint the bottom green. I thought, *whew! I can do this!* By the end of the day, you could clearly begin to see the sky, mountain range, and a grassy meadow. I did a good job with my green grass area, and I went back to the hotel feeling proud.

When we arrived the next day, Alfredo drew a big sun in the sky and told Greg and Lee to paint it. He gave the artist from USC the mountain range, then asked another college student and me to start working on the grass again. I breathed a sigh of re- lief—*I've still got this under control.* Towards the end of day two, Alfredo brought me a cup with black paint and a brush and said, "Come here, I want you to start on this." I eagerly followed him. He took the black paint and went over the line that separated the dark green and the lighter green. He instructed me how to do it. I stepped back and said, "No, I can't do that. I'm not good in art. I can only paint large spaces the same color. I will mess it up!" He put the cup in my hand and said, "You will not mess it up," and he walked away.

To tell you I was nervous is an understatement. I didn't cry, but I wanted to. I was so nervous with the black brush strokes. It looked so hard to me, and so final! I thought to myself, *I am going to screw this up, the whole team is going to be mad at me, and the poor kids are going to have to look at what the American messed up forever.* My fears from my non-artistic past were telling me lies, and I really wanted to stop. But I kept painting.

After the black line, Alfredo handed me a sponge and told me to paint a lighter green over the grass to give it depth. I started laughing and said, "I am a TERRIBLE sponge painter! I painted a bathroom in Virginia Beach with sponge paint, and it looked like someone splattered Pepto Bismol all over the walls. Alfredo once again told me, "You are not going to mess up." I went to grab some gloves, because I didn't want to get my fingers all dirty with the paint from the sponge. Alfredo looked at me and said, "What are those gloves for?" I replied, "I don't want to get my hands dirty." He laughed. Then he walked over, put his hands in the paint, then wiped them all over my hands and arms. He said, "Now you are already dirty, so you don't need gloves. Painting is messy. Get to painting."

Every so often, Alfredo would step in, make little corrections, tell me how to change my approach, then walk away. As I made my way down the long wall, I gained a little more confidence with each section, and started to relax a little. Occasionally,

Alfredo would walk behind me and say, "Good job," or "Beautiful." By the end of day two, you could start to see what Alfredo was creating, his vision. I nicknamed him the Master that day.

Day three, right out of the gate, Alfredo gave me a harder job. He wanted me to add tree bark on the trees. I instantly said, "No! I can't do that, it's so final." The technique involved taking plaster and putting it on the trees, then using the side of the spatula to add grooves to look like bark. Of course, just like when I was in kindergarten, I started looking at what the other people were doing, and how amazing their work looked. I instantly felt defeated. Alfredo did not listen to me. He took me down to the very end of the mural and said, "Start here." (He probably wanted to get me as far from the group as possible so I wouldn't compare.) So I started, very, very slowly. He would walk by and say things like, "It's too heavy, try this." Or "Use the tip like this, not the way you are doing it," then walk away. Later he would come back through and say, "Beautiful job!" or my favorite: "Perfect!" Hearing those words did so much for me.

By the end of day three, I was feeling good about the project. I noticed a few things about Alfredo. He was the master, and he didn't expect or need me to be a master. He only needed me to follow his lead.

He also didn't expect perfection from me, because he knew I was an amateur. He started me off with easy things to grow my confidence, then he would progress me on to the next level, which was a little harder. He left me there until I grew comfortable, and then he would take me to the next level. Most importantly of all, Alfredo didn't hover. He let me learn and grow, every so often giving guidance, always willing and open for me to ask questions. He encouraged me—not all the time, but when he saw fit. Alfredo was serious about his work. It wasn't a game to him. He had a picture in his mind, and he wanted us to follow his lead.

Day four was our last day, and we had to finish the project and add another layer of detail. Alfredo gave me black paint again. I hate black. It's so harsh and feels final. If you mess it up, it will be a BIG mess up. He told me to start outlining the trees, animals, and flowers. UGH! It was so nerve-racking, so deliberate, and it took so much time.

While I was outlining everything, I had a revelation. The wall was like our children: they come into the world a blank slate. There is a masterpiece behind each blank slate that only the Master knows in his mind. Like a master painter, God will guide us with each stroke, each phase. He will leave us with a task to accomplish, be available for our questions, and every so often give us encouraging words to keep us going. Each phase gets harder and harder, and it seems so tedious and hard! But we must trust the Master. There are lots of times we want to quit, walk away, and throw in the towel, but if we want to see the finished product, the fruits of our labor, we must stay on the wall and continue to paint and push through.

The Master doesn't hover or micro-manage us. He gives us the tools we need, and the direction, and He will teach us if we will listen, but that part is up to us.

He is always there, working not only with us, but with other people who are painting on the wall. He is just a few steps away, even though at times His distance feels like a mile. We, amateur painters, get insecure. But the Master builds us up, encourages us, gives us direction, and tells us we are doing a good job.

Here is the coolest part of all. Do you remember how Alfredo would always tell me, "You aren't going to mess it up?" He wasn't saying that because I

—

THE MASTER
BUILDS US UP,
ENCOURAGES
US, GIVE US
DIRECTION, AND
TELLS US WE
ARE DOING A
GOOD JOB.

—

was some great artist. I proved to you earlier that I have NO skills. Rather, he was saying that because HE was the Master! He knew that no matter what I did, he could fix it. No matter how badly I messed it up, the art would not be messed up forever. While we took our breaks, Alfredo would come behind us and put his masterful touches all over the painting. He would fill in the gaps, lighten the areas that were too dark, and darken the areas that were too light. He added shading and texture, and he added white to make certain things pop. He brought the mural to life. The master covered it all with his touch.

On my ride back to the hotel the last day, I kept thinking about how God is the Master, and His Grace covers all. We don't have to earn it, deserve it, or even understand it, but He covers all and He alone is holding us, moms, together. He will go behind us and fix our little masterpieces, our children. He will fill in the gaps, He will shade or lighten or take away. He will turn a mistake into a beautiful flower, because He is the Master.

Wow! What a picture! What an amazing God. He created a story in me, from kindergarten throughout my whole life, and brought it to a beautiful picture in Costa Rica. His lesson was clear as day to me:

He is the Master, and His grace covers me and all His children.

I wanted to share with you my story and revelation of the Master. I believe so much of motherhood is like my experience painting the mural in Costa Rica. Moms start off the journey a bit nervous about what to expect in motherhood and we feel a little inadequate to do the job, just like I felt inadequate to paint the mural. We want a plan, want to know what to expect, just like I wanted the plan from Alfredo. But, just as Alfredo did not give me a plan, God does not give us the plan of our journey of motherhood. He has a plan, but gives it to us in pieces, when the timing is right. We have a Master who knows what the painting of our child will look like, and He doesn't need us to know everything about motherhood. It's almost better that we don't, because if we knew everything, we wouldn't need a Master to help us along the way.

No, He has the blueprint of your child's life, and He knows the final look of your child's painting.

Follow His lead. Walk closely with Him, and keep in mind the entire journey that when you mess

—

REST IN
GOD'S
GRACE

—

up—and you will—the Master will come behind you and put His touch on your child. He will fill in all the gaps and make right what you can't. Accept His grace like a warm blanket on a cold winter's night. Allow God's sovereignty to cover you in your mothering and cover your child. You are in good hands! He's got you!

That is my story about God's grace. I share it with you because we all need grace, the unmerited favor of God. As a mom, you need to know that grace is abundant, free, and yours for the taking. Rest in God's grace.

CHAPTER TWO

CHAPTER TWO
What's the Plan?

*For you created my inmost being; you knit
me together in my mother's womb.*

PSALM 139:13

———

When we bring our new baby home from the hospital, none of us, new moms, know what we are doing, and it is a little scary. We want to know how to take care of the baby—when to let them cry and when to go in and get them, what is normal and what is a problem. Most of the time we are just "winging" it.

As my child grew, my insecurity as a mom grew as well. It felt like every time I started figuring out a stage of life, my child would only be in that stage for a few more months and then he or she would move on to the next stage, one that I didn't have a clue about either. Over and over again I had to start from the ground up. This pattern is still happening today. Now I'm learning how to navigate being a grandmother and a mother-in-law. I'm learning when to keep my mouth closed and when to step in to help. It is not as intuitive as you would think. Regardless of what stage my child is in, I always want to know what the plan is for my child. What should I be doing as a mom?

Sure, all my friends were in the same boat, and we would talk about what we were doing, what was working and what was not working. But no one ever truly knows, and there is no one-size-fits-all to raising kids. The good news that I want to share with you is that we don't have to know the plan. The Creator of our children knows the plan because He is the Creator and Master. Psalm 139:13 tells us that, "For you created my inmost being; you knit me together in my mother's womb." God is the Creator of our children, and He not only knows how they are wired, He knows their whole life from start to finish. As a mom, we would all be wise to stop worrying about what the plan is and start walking with our heavenly Father daily and seek His wisdom in raising our children.

LEARN TO LISTEN TO GOD'S VOICE

God is the Creator of our children, and He not only knows how they are wired, He knows their whole life from start to finish.

Like Alfredo, God has the plan, but He doesn't share it with us. If He did, we might worry and fret, lose hope, or go off and think we could do it on our own. But if we seek a relationship with the Creator, He will give us direction each step of the way. We will begin to learn His voice and to follow after Him. The Bible tells us that we are His sheep and the sheep follow the shepherd: "My sheep listen to my voice; I know them, and they follow me" (John 10:27). As a mom, learn how to listen to God's voice. In order to develop that skill, you must slow down your pace of life and quiet all the noise around you. I learned how to do that during my quiet time, meeting with God every morning, hopefully before the children woke up. That was my time with God, to get the "plan" for the day. Just like I constantly went to Alfredo on the wall, I went to God each morning, giving Him my day, offering it to Him. I would lay my desires and dreams before the Lord, telling Him what I had in mind for the day, but always tried to be open to His idea for my day. In those early mornings that is where I hit "reset" in my life. God's plan was usually simple, given to me either through a devotional, reading my Bible or a thought I would have while journaling. God guided me and showed me that I could not manufacture patience for my child, that was a fruit of the Spirit and came with walking with Him.

Our children come into this world as a blank slate, or to follow our analogy, a blank wall. The Master has the mural in His mind, and He begins to make the sketches and draw the outlines that will be the foundation of the painting. We, as moms, should be listening to the Master and following His direction as we parent our sweet children, because He knows what the final work of art will look like.

You might be thinking, "I don't ever hear God." My question to you is, do you know Him? He is readily available to us all, regardless of what our past looks like or how much education you have. He wants a relationship with all of us. In Revelation 3:20 He says, "Here I am! I stand at the door and knock. If anyone hears my voice and opens the door, I will come in and eat with that person, and they with me." Jesus is ready and willing to have a relationship with you. The phrase "will come in and eat" indicates that He is looking for an intimate relationship. You eat with your friends, with loved ones, with people that you enjoy hanging out with. That is what Jesus wants from us—a close relationship so that when we hear His voice, we know it and follow His direction.

If you want to know the plan, get to know Jesus. He will give you the plan one day at a time.

The best way to get to know Jesus is to read the Bible. If you don't know where to start, start in the book of John. It is a great, easy-to-read book that will take you through the life of Jesus on this earth. When you finish John, start at the beginning of the Bible in Genesis and read all the way through. Reading the Bible from cover to cover will give you a clear picture of who God is—His sovereignty, power, and deep love for ALL of us! Years ago, I decided to read the Bible all the way through. It took me a while, I didn't follow a plan, just started to read. Some days I would only read a chapter and another day I would read several chapters. I didn't put a time limit on myself, I just started reading. What I found was that God is a loving God, a patient God, that obedience is a BIG deal to Him. I also loved learning the sovereignty of God, how God had a plan from the beginning of time. I also learned that God is long suffering with His people.

I believe, as moms, one reason we want to know the plan ahead of time is because we want to know when or if the road will be bumpy. We want to know how to avoid the hard parts of life. But you can't avoid the hard parts of life. Everyone has them, and everyone has to go through them. That is just the way life is. I know that, as a mom, you want to protect your children from every harmful situation. But trust me, you can't. That is just life. Jesus tells us in John 16:33,

In this world you will have trouble. But take heart! I have overcome the world.

Trouble is unavoidable. What is a mom to do? Once again, trust the Lord. He has the plan, so lean into Him. Fear not, because He has overcome the world. Jesus is bigger than any problem, sickness, divorce, adoption, fostering situation, or evil that you may encounter, and through Him you will get through any bump in the road.

Our desire to know the plan is not just limited to parenting our children. I want to know the plan with my finances, job search, health, relationships, and how my children are going to turn out. I want to know what areas my children are going to struggle with so I can be prepared—or avoid the "bad" all together. But, like I said it doesn't work that way. Even when we think we are on the right track, doing all we can be doing, sometimes life throws us a curve ball, something we don't think we will ever be able to handle.

I learned this firsthand when my daughter Kelsey was four years old and got very sick. She spiked a high fever, and it took multiple trips to the hospital and doctor's office before we found out she had kidney reflux. She went on medicine and every year had to be tested with a VCUG test (a highly invasive test that is not pleasant). I was doing everything the doctors told me to do, giving Kelsey medicine every day and taking her to the doctor on schedule. When she was six years old, they told me we didn't need to do the VCUG because she was doing so well. But when I took her in for her seven-year appointment, they told me that her kidneys were not doing well at all, and her right kidney was the size of a four year old's kidney. Talk about panic! I wanted to know the plan. I wanted someone to tell me she was going to be okay, that her kidney was not damaged for life. I eventually got my answers, and she eventually had surgery to fix the problem.

My point is, God walked me through every step of the way and He will do the same for you. You want to know the plan?

Get to know your heavenly Father, and He will guide your steps.

He knows the plan. He will walk with you every step of the way and will not leave you. That doesn't mean He will make everything turn out the way you want it, but He will be with you.

CHAPTER THREE

CHAPTER THREE
Life Is Messy

I have told you these things, so that in me you may
have peace. In this world you will have trouble.
But take heart! I have overcome the world.

JOHN 16:33

———

Sometimes life does not turn out the way we want it to. That's life, right? When we first became moms, we had beautiful images in our mind of how motherhood will be—or at least I did. I thought I would be the best mom ever, always nurturing, loving, and caring. I would be wonderful at discipline, but I would probably never have to really discipline my children because they would be little angels. I wasn't going to be the mom that had "bad" kids. No, my children were going to be beautiful, delightful in every way, and never give me any trouble. At some point in my mothering experience, I woke up out of my daze and realized my daydreams were just that—dreams— and life is not like a dream or a movie. Life is real, and it doesn't always work out the way I think it should. Above all else, life is messy!

When I painted that mural in Costa Rica, I learned that painting is messy. When Alfredo had me sponge painting, he wouldn't let me wear gloves because he knew that the best results come when we allow ourselves to get dirty in the process of creating. I have found in being a mom that children are messy too. I'm not just talking making a mess with crayons, or spilled paint, or dirt on their shoes or clothes, I'm talking about life with children is messy. Life in general is not always a pretty picture, and we cannot wear gloves to keep the grime of the world off of our hands. Life with children will bring tears, both from the child and the mom. Life with children will bring hardship, at times sadness and poor or unwise choices. But, that is life.

Failing to embrace the mess of parenting is sort of like standing at the edge of the ocean and asking the tide to not come in. It's coming, and you can either enjoy it or be extremely frustrated the whole time while it is inching towards you. Moms, listen, I get it. I love a well-run house and well-behaved children just like the rest of you. But the bottom line is, children are children. They are human. Children are going to not mind you. They are not going to do what you want them to do or behave the way you want them to behave, because at the end of the day, they are children. We have two choices as moms: we can embrace the fact that our children are not

Greg and Alfredo

COSTA RICA

perfect, roll up our sleeves, and start parenting, or we can be in a constant state of frustration, wondering why these things are happening and constantly striving for perfection that will never be achieved. We will frustrate and repel our children in the process. Which one do you want? I choose a little mess. I choose to roll up my sleeves, put my big girl panties on, and start being a mom who knows my child is not perfect, I am not perfect, and I might as well embrace the mess of life. Embrace the thought, I am not a perfect mom, parenting a not perfect child, but we are perfectly paired together by God.

I think one reason I shy away from messy situations is that I don't want to deal with a mess that gets so big that I can't ever "fix" it. That is what I was afraid of with Alfredo and the mural, and if I'm honest, that is what I'm afraid of with my children. You know what I'm talking about—when your two or three-year-old pitches a royal fit, and you are tired, you just want to look the other way and justify everything. You give excuses: "He's tired, he is getting sick, he missed his nap today, there is a full moon tonight." The list goes on and on.

It doesn't stop in the toddler years. When your child is in elementary school and starts developing an "attitude" you've never seen before, you may try

—

LIFE IS
MESSY!
EMBRACE
THE MESS!

—

to blame the school, your child's friends, or anyone else in sight—anything to avoid accepting the reality that your child is growing up and pushing the boundaries. It's normal, and it's messy. It's also embarrassing at times, especially when the attitude rears its ugly head around your parents or in-laws or your friends. Once again, roll up your sleeves, wipe a little war paint on your face, and get messy. Embrace it! Start doing the real work of parenting.

Keep going: teen years, same situation, just accelerated a bit, now the "attitude" has a voice, and a loud one at that. Everything seems to be a bigger deal than it should be, threats are made and sometimes executed. As a mom, this is the BIG mess that we all dread. We don't want to roll up our sleeves and get to work with a teenager because it is so difficult, discouraging, and heart-wrenching at times. It's so much easier to put your head in the sand, look the other way, or think to yourself, "I only have one year left until they go to college, I'll just bide my time." But, that doesn't work. Life is messy. Being a mom is messy.

What is a mom to do? Here are a few pointers that will apply regardless of your child's age:

• Embrace the Mess.
Realize that in this world you WILL have trouble,

but you don't have to fear because Jesus has overcome the world (John 16:33). Nothing will change on its own; it takes work. Children take work. You are not going to escape it, whether they are toddlers or teenagers. Be the parent. Teach them, discipline them, love them, nurture them, listen to them, empathize with them, correct them, and above all else, don't give up on them!

• Realize that no mess is so big it can't be cleaned up. Seriously! Your heavenly Father specializes in the messes that are so big, so out of control that you can't handle them on your own. He offers redemption and grace for every situation. Get on your knees. Pray and seek God, asking for wisdom and guidance to raise your children. I've even seen God bring healing and restoration to families who are working through an unplanned teenage pregnancy. No problem is too big, no situation is beyond His control to bring healing and restoration. Don't give up!

• Find joy in the mess.
You don't have to love your situation to find joy, but finding joy might just be the factor that gets you through it. When I was painting the mural, Alfredo didn't hover over me, correcting my every paint stroke. He gave me room to experiment, to mess up, to figure a few things out. He would periodical-

ly walk behind me and say ever so quietly, "Good job," "Beautiful," "Excellent," "Good work," "Try it this way," "Don't be so heavy here." Then Alfredo would walk away again and leave me to my masterpiece.

Alfredo was not only interested in the finished product, he was also interested in me as the painter. He wanted to instruct me, guide me, uplift me, and encourage me on the journey of painting the wall. The same is true of our heavenly Father. He is not only interested in our child and the finished product; He wants to build us moms up in the process. He wants to teach us, guide us, uplift us, encourage us, and tell us we are doing a great job. I believe it is in the messy journey of motherhood that I have grown the most as a woman and in my faith journey with God. I have learned to listen for His voice, His direction, when I am on my knees crying out to Him for the answers. He doesn't hover over me. He gives me room to make mistakes or make the right choice, and then He comes in behind me and whispers in my ear, "try this," "that was too harsh, too permissive," "well done," "relax, I've got this." Those are the times I have grown the most and gained confidence in being a mom. That is where the joy is, my friends.

There have been many times in parenting where

I have been so lost, not knowing what to do, and everything I was doing felt like a disaster. I remember when Abby was in high school and we were constantly butting heads. My husband, Greg, seemed to speak the "Abby" language, but while I used to speak fluent "Abby," I had lost my touch. It was a very discouraging time for me as a mom. Ironically, this was right when my ministry, Birds on a Wire, was just starting to be successful. You better believe the enemy—Satan—was constantly whispering in my ear. His whispers were lies straight from the pit of hell, but lies that I would listen to. "Why are you leading a mom's ministry? You are a hot mess with Abby. You can't even get along with her. Who do you think you are? You are a hypocrite." Thankfully I had been parenting long enough to know those were lies.

I got on my knees and cried out to God for help! Help me with this child of mine, the one I love and adore, but right now I cannot say "Good morning" to without us getting into an argument. I cried out to God and asked for wisdom. I ended up going to a personality coach in our area, a woman who specializes in the different temperaments. Mind you, these are the same temperaments that I stood on the stage and spoke about. I would tell all the moms to be a student of your child. I would share how learning the temperaments changed my life as a mom with Taylor (and it did). But, now, years later, I needed help to understand Abby. To say that I had to eat some humble pie was an understatement. Life is messy, and when you roll up your sleeves and start to parent, you are going to get messy and you will probably have to eat humble pie at some point.

Abby and I met with the personality coach together a few times, and in that room I learned how to better parent my very red, choleric daughter. I learned why she was getting so angry with me, and how I had been hurting her with my very yellow, sanguine temperament without even realizing it. We both learned so much about each other, and things started to change. It took a while, but I was overjoyed to see even subtle changes. I will give full disclosure and let you know that it wasn't until Abby went to college that our relationship really healed. But even before that, we did have longer periods of "good" times together. Greg still spoke fluent Abby, and I still did not, but I learned to be thankful that he spoke her language and that at least one of us was on her page at all times.

Life is messy, moms. There is no escaping it. Roll up those sleeves, dig in, and get to work!

—

I'M NOT A
PERFECT MOM,
BUT I WAS
PERFECTLY
PAIRED FOR
YOU BY GOD

—

CHAPTER FOUR

CHAPTER FOUR
Is This Parenting Thing Getting Harder?

*Then you will know the truth, and the truth
will set you free.*

JOHN 8:32

———

Painting the wall started off easy. Alfredo assigned all of us our specific jobs and we got to work. My job was to take the dark green paint that Alfredo put together and take my paintbrush and swirl it onto the wall over and over again until the entire lower third of the wall was swirly, twirly green.

About three-fourths of the way through my first assignment, I finally started to relax and enjoy myself. I started to get the hang of things and was feeling confident in my approach. I was laughing and talking with my team and really enjoying myself. When I got to the end of the wall, I did what every painter would do: I went to the Master and asked what the next job was going to be. Alfredo looked at me, started whistling, and walked over to his paint station. He poured several different colors together and gave me a sponge. We walk over to the wall, and after he wiped wet paint all over my hands, he taught me how to sponge paint the new greenish color on the lower third of the wall. Now I had a new task, with a new technique, and I once again felt a little flustered, incompetent, and unsure of what I was doing.

When I told Alfredo I couldn't do the sponge technique, he laughed and said, "Yes you can," and walked away. Once again, he left me to it. Every so often he would walk behind me, give me some instructions, whisper "Good job" or "Beautiful," and walk away. Once again, about three-fourths of the way through working on the wall, I started to feel comfortable, gained a little confidence, and started to relax. When I got to the end of the sponge part, I was feeling good about myself as an artist. I looked down the wall and saw that the picture was starting to come together. I was feeling good about my role on the wall, and felt like I had my act together. This time, when I went to Alfredo to ask him what my next assignment was, I had more confidence. I was almost excited to hear about my next job.

When I asked Alfredo what was next, he continued to whistle, walked over to the paint station, and grabbed a medium-sized brush and some black paint. He took the paintbrush, dipped it into the black paint, and said, "Do this with the black paint" while making a line between the two shades of green grass that separated section two and three of the wall. Then he said, "after you draw the line, take the side of your palm and rub it off. This leaves a shading effect." What do you think I said in response? "I don't want to do that job! It is with black paint, so it feels permanent, and I will mess it up." Alfredo smiled at me and started to walk off, saying, "You aren't going to mess it up!" He kept walking away. I began to draw the black line all the way down the wall and rubbing it off with my hand, just like I was instructed to do.

With each phase of the mural, the tasks kept getting harder and harder. The drill was the same. Each time, I felt very insecure about the new task, but I toughed it out, and about three quarters of the way through I felt like I was getting the hang of it. Then I was introduced to a new job.

I felt especially unqualified when we got to the tree bark. Alfredo took plaster and a straight edge and asked us to wipe the plaster on the trunk of the tree. After we did that, we would quickly take the straight edge, turn it on its side, and make lines down the tree trunk to look like lines in tree bark. It was a cool concept when I was watching a college student do it on a tree. But when Alfredo gave me my batch, I instantly felt inadequate. The plaster felt more permanent. It would dry fairly quickly, and it was hard to fix it if you messed up. That didn't seem to matter to Alfredo. He wasn't interested that I was not an artist, had no apparent skill in art, and was woefully insecure. He kept pushing me to move on to the next phase with the words, "You aren't going to mess it up."

The last part of painting the wall was taking black paint and outlining most of the mural. This was a tedious and time-consuming job. As a painter, you had to be still and have a steady hand. At times, you just had to walk away to loosen up a bit. This section of the mural reminded me so much of those teen years in parenting. There are lots of conversations, lots of tears, lots of sleepless nights thinking about what you are doing wrong as a parent or wondering how to get your teenager to listen to you. But no matter how hard and tedious it gets, just like the mural, you need to stick with it and not walk away and give up. Outlining the picture in black is what makes the mural pop. Likewise, parenting during the teen years will try your patience, but I promise you that you will be glad you put the work in and didn't give up.

We begin our journey of motherhood apprehensive, insecure, and unsure of what to do, but we start. We figure it out as we go. We muddle through those first few nights, weeks, months—and with each passing day we gain a little more confidence. Just when we feel like we have a good handle on things with our child, they change. They drop a nap, drop a feeding, start teething, get their first cold or ear infection, and now all of a sudden we are in the dark again. This process never stops. Just when you figure out what method of discipline works for them they grow into the next stage. With each stage comes new challenges, more difficult challenges. They enter pre-school or kindergarten and are introduced to "friends" that you have not hand selected for them, friends who have influence. As a mom, you start to panic and feel insecure again. What if you've lost all your influence and it's going downhill from here? Don't panic, but it only gets worse! With each stage, with each transition, the stakes are upped and you, as a mom, feel as if you are starting over. It continues even when your children grow into adults, and you become a grandmother. But don't lose hope.

Now that you feel as if your anxiety is through the roof, let me tell you a few things that will bring your blood pressure down a little.

You don't have to know everything!

God knows what is coming down the pipe, and He will guide you all the way. Not only will He guide you along the way, He wants to guide you. Psalms 23, a familiar passage for most of us, says,

The Lord is my shepherd, I lack nothing.
He makes me lie down in green pastures,
he leads me beside quiet waters,
he refreshes my soul.
He guides me along the right paths
for his name's sake.
Even though I walk
through the darkest valley,
I will fear no evil,
for you are with me;
your rod and your staff,
they comfort me.
You prepare a table before me
in the presence of my enemies.
You anoint my head with oil;
my cup overflows.
Surely your goodness and love will follow me
all the days of my life,
and I will dwell in the house of the Lord
forever.

It also says in Proverbs 3:5-6,

Trust in the Lord with all your heart and lean not on your own understanding; in all your ways submit to him, and he will make your paths straight.

These verses are not just sweet stories in an ancient book, they are truth. And Jesus told us that the *"truth will set you free"* (John 8:32). Take heart in the fact that God knows the entire plan, and in due time, He will guide you.

• *There is no mess that God cannot make right.*
I know we believe at times that some things in this world are beyond repair, some people are beyond repair. But that is not true. Jesus is the Savior of this world. He came to bring restoration, healing, and redemption. As a mom, it doesn't matter how bad you make a situation, God can fix it. Remember Romans 8:28: "And we know that in all things God works for the good of those who love him, who have been called according to his purpose." Did you catch that? All things work together for good. It doesn't say "sometimes" or "maybe," it says "all things." Do you believe that? Do you trust God? He is trustworthy, even with your precious children.

• *God loves your children more than you do.*

He will pursue them throughout their whole life because He loves them. There is nothing they can do that will make Him not love them. John 3:16 tells us, "For God so loved the world that he gave his one and only Son, that whoever believes in him shall not perish but have eternal life." You may be reading this book, and your child has gone off the deep end. I'm talking drugs, rebellion, and running as far from God as he or she possibly can. Mom, you need to know this fact: God loves your child. God is and will continue to pursue your child. Don't lose hope. Keep praying, keep seeking God, and keep your eyes focused on Him.

Alfredo and my son Taylor

COSTA RICA

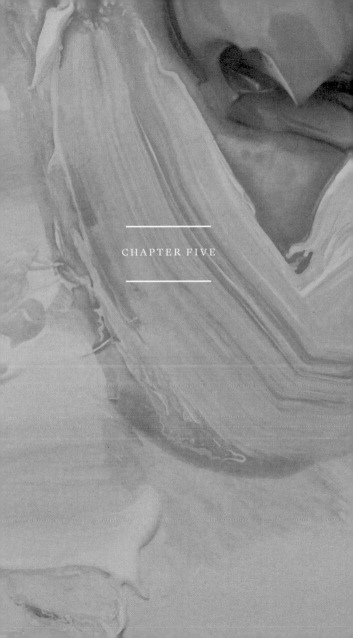

CHAPTER FIVE

The Final Masterpiece

He tends his flock like a shepherd:
He gathers the lambs in his arms
and carries them close to his heart;
he gently leads those that have young.

ISAIAH 40:11

On the last day of painting the mural, a beautiful thing happened for me as a painter. I finally realized the importance of having a Master artist behind the mural. Alfredo was an experienced painter. This was not his first time painting a huge mural—he was a professional. The reason that he stayed so calm throughout the process was because of his ability, skill set, and talent, not because of our team's talent. He knew that he had the talent to "fix" anything we messed up, and he did. When we were at lunch, eating a snack, or taking a break, Alfredo would go behind us and fill in all our mistakes. He would highlight certain areas, darken others, he would shade and fill in everything that we missed. Alfredo put his final touches on the mural, and those touches made the entire wall come to life.

Once again, the mural parallels Jesus as the Master in guiding us in motherhood. Jesus walks with us, gently guiding us (Isaiah 40:11) as we lead and parent our children. He doesn't need us to be a master at mothering, and doesn't expect that of us. Moms, here's the point: Jesus is the Master painter in your child's life. I know you feel insecure at times, like you don't know what you are doing because this is the first time you've parented this toddler, eight-year-old, middle schooler, high schooler, or college student, and you are scared out of your mind that you are going to mess your child up. That is where Jesus comes in and does what only Jesus can do: "fix" your mistakes. He goes behind us and uses everything we did, right or wrong, to make our child what He created them to be. He fills in the gaps, heals deep wounds, restores relationships, and redeems the brokenhearted. He is the Master, the Savior. His grace covers our mistakes. Grace is a beautiful concept that most of us, including me, skip over. Jesus covered us with His blood at the cross, and His grace covers our mistakes.

What is grace again? Grace is the free (Romans 3:24), unmerited favor of God. It costs us nothing, and there is nothing we can do to earn it (Ephesians 2:8-9). Favor means that God adores you! He sees you, loves you, and is proud of you. You are His child! Through Jesus, He has covered you. Covered

—

"MY GRACE IS
SUFFICIENT
FOR YOU, FOR
MY POWER IS
MADE PERFECT
IN WEAKNESS."

2 CORINTHIANS 12:9

—

you in ALL your mistakes. Jesus said, "My grace is sufficient" (2 Corinthians 12:9). You are the exact mom that God chose for your child, whether you are the birth mom, adopted mom, or foster mom. You are a work in progress, and so is your child. God is at work behind the scenes, and He will carry you and your children to a complete and beautiful masterpiece in the end.

As our time together comes to a close, I want to encourage you as a mom to trust in your heavenly Father and to seek a relationship with Him. Trust Jesus to guide you and give you wisdom when you need it most. It is not up to you to create a beautiful masterpiece in your child—that is Jesus' role. Your role is to follow Him, listen to His voice, and stay in step with Him along this journey of motherhood. Leave the finished masterpiece to the Master.

About the Author

Karen Stubbs is the founder and leader of Birds on a Wire, a ministry designed to equip moms through truth, encouragement and community. She is the author of three books, Letters to Moms, Moments with God and Tips on Motherhood. She has also developed small group curricula for moms that is being used across 50 states and in 36 countries. Karen is the wife of Greg Stubbs, they have four grown children and resides in Cumming, Ga.

After graduating from Auburn University, she and Greg moved to Virginia Beach where Greg served in the Navy as a fighter pilot. It was during those tough early years that Karen, as a young mom, gained her passion for motherhood and grew in her reliance on God. She is passionate about challenging moms to experience motherhood in the way God intended it for them and their families.